LIGHT MAGIC!

Most magic tricks would be pretty useless without light. Light enables us to see, and gives our world colour. Light is amazingly versatile. It can pass straight through some substances, and causes ghostly reflections when it bounces off others. Light is a natural magician that can fool us into seeing things that just aren't there. Is it an optical illusion or is it just a trick of the light?

BE AN EXPERT MAGICIAN

PREPARING YOUR ROUTINE

There is much more to being a magician than just doing tricks. It is important that you and your assistant practise your whole routine lots of times, so that your performance goes smoothly when you do it for real. You will be a more entertaining magician if you do.

PROPS

Props are all the bit and pieces of equipment that a magician uses during an act. This includes your clothes as well as the tricks themselves. It's a good idea to make a magician's trunk from a large box to keep all your props in. During your routine you can dip into the trunk, pulling out all sorts of equipment and crazy objects (see Distraction). You could also tell jokes about these objects.

PROPS LIST

Magic wand
Top hat
Waistcoat
Silk scarves
Balloons
Paint
Boxes
Containers
Food colouring
Paper

Wax
candle
Cardboard
Eggs
Wire
Tissue paper
Sticky tape
Mirrors
Cellophane

Marker
pen
Coins

WHICH TRICKS?
Work out which tricks you want to put in your routine. Put in some long tricks and some short tricks.

WARNING: For one of the tricks in this book you need to light a candle. Be very careful that it does not set light to anything.

MAGICIAN'S PATTER
Patter is what you say during your routine. Good patter makes a routine

much more interesting and allows it to run much more smoothly. It is a good way to entertain your audience during the slower parts of your routine. Try to make up a story for each trick. Practise your patter when you practise your tricks.

DISTRACTION
Distraction is an important part of a magician's routine. By waving a colourful scarf in the air or telling a joke, you can take an audience's attention away from something you'd rather they didn't see!

KEEP IT SECRET
The best magicians never give away their secrets. If anyone asks how your tricks work, just reply "By magic!" Then you can impress people with your tricks again and again.

INTRODUCING MAGIC MANDY
AND THE
VANISHING COIN

Magic Mandy makes the coin disappear with her amazing magic rings!

WHAT YOU NEED
*Wrapping paper
(preferably with a
random pattern)
Thin card
Gold paint
Small coin*

Ask to borrow a coin from the audience. Put it on the patterned paper. Now put the white circle over the "spoof" ring and put the real ring on top. Pick up this pile and put it over the coin. Take off the real ring and white circle — the coin has disappeared! Put the circle and ring back and remove the pile. Suddenly the coin is back!

THE SCIENCE BENEATH THE TRICK

When the coin is covered by the ring with the patterned paper underneath it, the coin is hidden. But both rings look 'see-through' to the audience when they are laid on the paper. They think that they are seeing two proper rings because they see what they think they should see! The ring hides the edge of the circle of patterned paper, which would give the secret away if it could be seen.

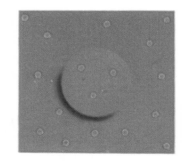

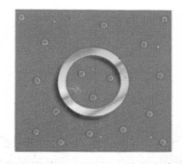

1 Make two rings about 8 cm across and paint them gold. Glue a circle of the patterned paper under one. Make a circle of white card the same size.

2 Find some wrapping paper with a random pattern on it, or paint a random pattern on plain paper.

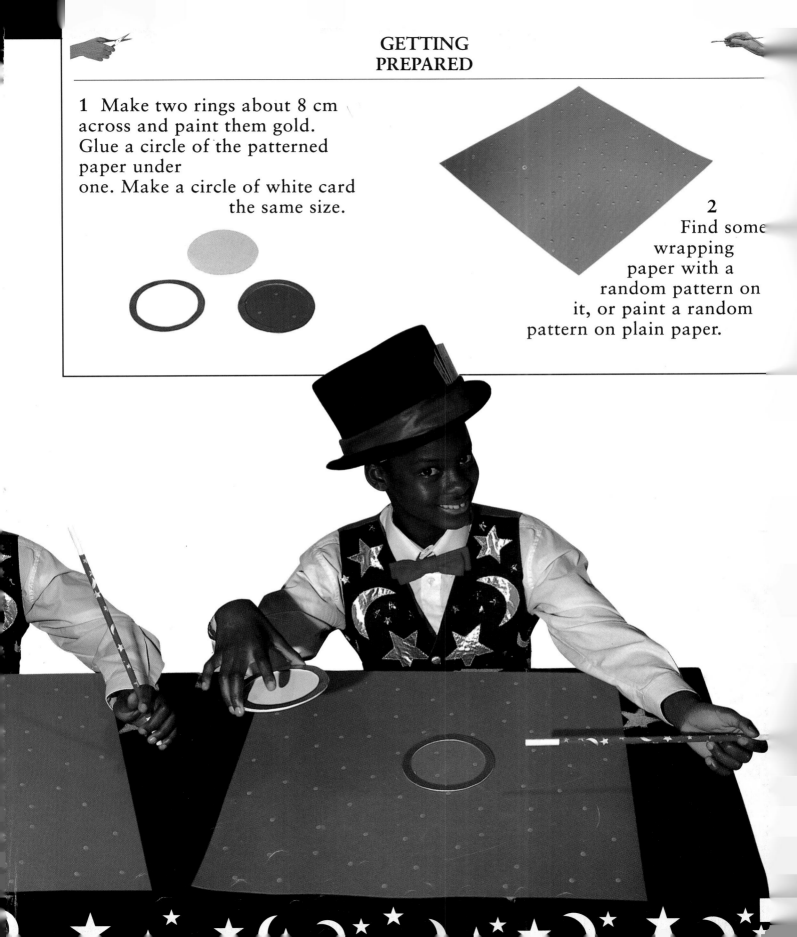

INTRODUCING MAGIC MEG
AND THE
GHOSTLY TUBE

The audience gasps as Magic Meg pulls scarves from the empty tube.

Before you start your act, put silk scarves or tissue papers into the secret compartment. Hold the tube up to your audience so that they can see your face through it. This proves that it's empty. Now stand it up on the table with the secret compartment pointing upwards. Produce the scarves with a flourish.

WHAT YOU NEED
Thin card
Coloured paper
Silk scarves or tissue
paper
Sticky tape

THE SCIENCE BEHIND THE TRICK

When you look along a long straight road or railway line, the sides of the road or the tracks seem to meet in the distance. This effect is called linear perspective, and we expect it to happen. When your audience looks through the ghost tube, they think the sides look closer because of perspective, so they do not notice the secret compartment.

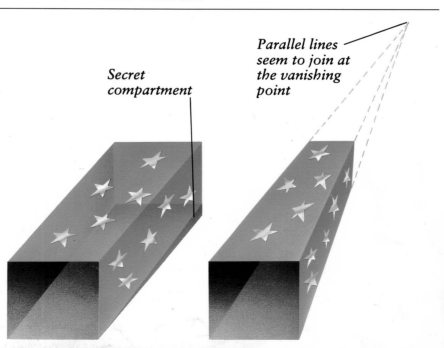

Secret compartment

Parallel lines seem to join at the vanishing point

10

GETTING PREPARED

1 Use card to make a tube about 10 cm square and 40 cm long. Glue another piece card inside to make a secret compartment.

2 Decorate the tube and stuff the compartment with scarves or tissue.

INTRODUCING MAGIC MEG
AND THE
AMAZING BLACK BOX

The audience gasp as Magic Meg pulls plants from thin air.

Before you start your act, load plants into the black cylinder and put the white cylinder and box over it. Lift out the white cylinder and show the audience that it is empty. Put it back and do the same with the box. The audience will think that both are empty.

WHAT YOU NEED
Thick card
Thin card (black and white)
Coloured card
Paints
Sticky tape

THE SCIENCE
BEHIND THE TRICK

This trick works because the black cylinder blends in with the black inside the box. The bars help to hide the shape of the black cylinder. The audience think the box is empty. Magicians call this effect "black art". Because black doesn't reflect much light, it is hard to tell one area from another.

Black cylinder is hidden inside the white one

The black cylinder is difficult to see from the front and the box seems to be empty

1 Make a cylinder about 30 cm high and about 12 cm across out of black card. Make a white cylinder, slightly taller and wider than the black, one to fit over it.

2 Make a square tube from thick card, the same height as the white cylinder and slightly wider, so that the white cylinder fits in it. Cut a hole in the front and add bars as shown. Decorate the box.

INTRODUCING MAGIC MILDRED
AND THE
MIRRORED BOX

For his next trick, Magic Mildred shows a box that is both empty and full!

Before you do the trick, load some silk scarves (or other objects) into the top of the box. Place the box on your table with the front flap pointing towards the audience. Open the front flap so that the audience can see inside. The box will look empty to them. Close it again, open the top flap and produce the silk scarves.

WHAT YOU NEED
Cardboard boxes
Rectangular glass
Coloured card
Silk scarves

THE SCIENCE BEHIND THE TRICK

The mirror inside the box is at an angle of 45 degrees. When you look through the flap in the front of the box, you see the floor of the box and its reflection, in the mirror above it. This makes the reflection look like the back of the box.

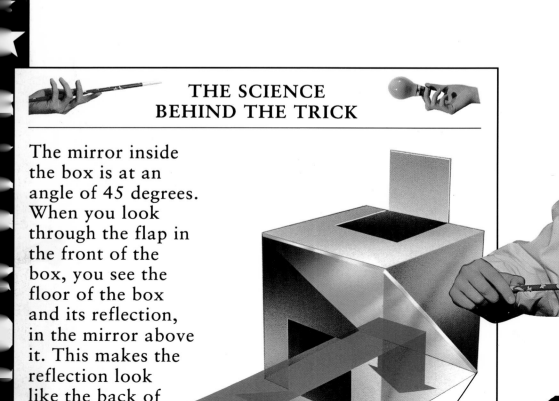

Light

Mirror

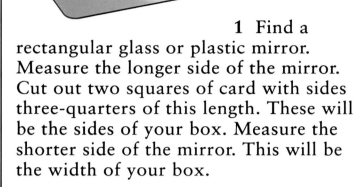

2 Make up the box with the mirror inside it (the mirror goes from the front-top edge to the bottom-back edge with the mirrored side pointing down. Cut flaps as shown, and decorate the box.

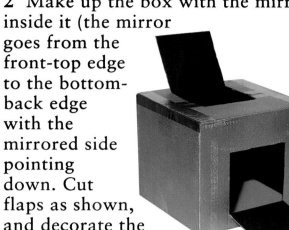

1 Find a rectangular glass or plastic mirror. Measure the longer side of the mirror. Cut out two squares of card with sides three-quarters of this length. These will be the sides of your box. Measure the shorter side of the mirror. This will be the width of your box.

INTRODUCING MAGIC MARVIN
AND THE
ENLARGING TUNNEL

It's weird! As Magic Marvin moves the egg further away into the tunnel, it just gets bigger and bigger!

WHAT YOU NEED
Thick white card
Sticky tape
Black marker pen
Sheet of black card
Two eggs the same size

Make sure that you put the enlarging tunnel where the audience will be looking straight into it. Pick up your two eggs and place them into the tunnel, one near the front and the other near the back. Ask a volunteer to say which one is biggest. Now remove both eggs and give them to your volunteer who will be amazed to find that they are the same size.

THE SCIENCE
BEHIND THE TRICK

The enlarging tunnel works by tricking the eye — it's an optical illusion. We think that the far end of the tunnel looks smaller than the front because of perspective, and do not suspect that it actually is much smaller. This makes an object appear to get bigger as it moves further back into the tunnel. Quite the opposite to what we expect to see!

1 Cut this shape out of card (50 cm long by 20 cm at the widest end).

2 Mark out the pattern with a pencil and ruler and then colour in the squares as shown. Make three more shapes and tape them together to make a tunnel.

3 Make a stand from black card. The tunnel fits into the hole.

17

INTRODUCING MAGIC MARCIA
AND THE
BENDING WIRE

What strange potion is it that bends solid wire for Magic Marcia?

Slide a piece of straight wire gradually into the potion — it will begin to look bent. Remove it and its straight again! The second time, let the wire hit the bottom, and keep pressing until it does bend. The audience will think the magic potion has bent it!

WHAT YOU NEED
Stiff wire (you should be able to bend it quite easily)
Tall glass
Water
Food colouring

THE SCIENCE BEHIND THE TRICK

When you put the wire into the water, it does not really bend, it just looks bent. This is caused by an effect called refraction. Light coming from the wire above the water goes straight into your eyes, but light from under the water changes direction when it goes through the glass and into the air. This makes the wire appear to be in a different place than it really is.

As the light changes direction through the water the wire appears to bend

1 Make some coloured water by adding a few drops of food colouring to a tumbler of water. Don't make the colour too dark because you need to see the wire through it.

2 You will also need to cut a piece of thin wire about 30 centimetres long. Ask an adult to help you cut the wire with a pair of pliers. You could use part of a wire coat-hanger.

WHAT YOU NEED
Clear plastic or glass
Glass of water
Candle

INTRODUCING MAGIC MIRIAM
AND THE
UNDERWATER CANDLE
Magic Miriam defies the laws of science to make a candle burn underwater!

Light the candle, open the side of the box and slide the candle into position (mark the right position before you start). The audience will be amazed to see something they've never seen before – a candle burning underwater.

WARNING: Be careful with fire. Make sure that the candle is not too near the box, and remember to blow it out after the trick.

THE SCIENCE
BEHIND THE TRICK

The glass panel lets light from the glass of water through so that the audience can see it from the other side. Some of the light from the candle passes through the glass as well, but some is reflected back, making it appear to be inside the glass. This effect is used to make ghosts appear on stage during plays — it's called Pepper's Ghost.

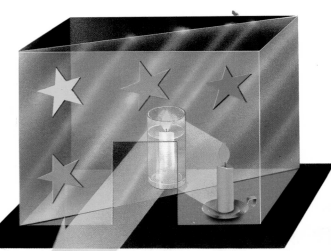

As light from the candle is reflected off the piece of glass, its image appears to hover in the glass of water

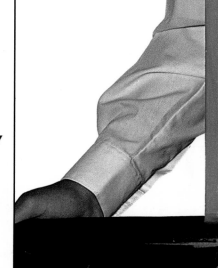

20

1 Paint the inside of a cardboard box black and attach it to a base.

2 Find a sheet of clear plastic or glass which will fit diagonally across the box.

3 Now cut a door in front of the box and decorate the box with symbols. Position the glass of water behind the glass partition and mark the place where the candle should go.

INTRODUCING MAGIC MIRIAM
AND THE
MAGIC TORCH

Magic Miriam stuns her audience with this illuminating trick!

For this trick you need a darkened room. Ask your assistant to turn off the lights. Cover the torch with the red filter and turn it on. Ask a volunteer to choose one of the coins and put it in the envelope. Pick up the envelope, which will look black. Turn off the torch, swap the red filter for the green one and turn on the torch to reveal the coin.

WHAT YOU NEED
Torch
Selection of coins
Cellophane

THE SCIENCE
BEHIND THE TRICK

The light that comes out of a torch is called white light. It is made up of lots of different colours of light. The cellophane only lets through the red or green parts of the white light. It stops all the other colours. When red light shines on the green cellophane, it is prevented from passing through, so the cellophane looks black. The green light can go through, so the coin can be seen.

Red light can't pass through the green cellophane

As green light passes through the green filter, the coin appears

1 Measure across the front of your torch. Make four identical frames from card, large enough to fit

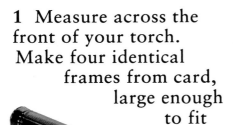

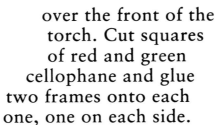

over the front of the torch. Cut squares of red and green cellophane and glue two frames onto each one, one on each side.

2 Make an envelope out of green cellophane. You should be able to put a coin in it and close it

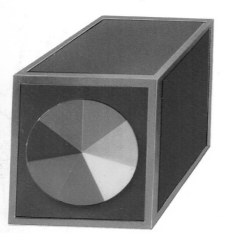

INTRODUCING MAGIC MARVIN
AND THE
CRAZY COLOUR WHEEL

Magic Marvin's magic wheel mixes the rainbow colours to conjure white.

Put the colour wheel on your magic table with the front facing the audience. In your patter, ask the audience to name all the colours on the wheel. Now announce that you will turn them all white. Wave your magic wand, spin the handle faster and faster, and the wheel will eventually turn white. Stop the wheel to get the colours back.

WHAT YOU NEED
Cardboard box
Thick card
Thin card
Plastic lid
Wooden dowel

THE SCIENCE
BEHIND THE TRICK

The light that comes from the Sun is white light. It's made up from lots of different colours, called the colours of the spectrum. When the wheel spins, your eyes are fooled into mixing the colours.

GETTING PREPARED

1 Paint and decorate a cardboard box, or make a box from thick card. Make small holes in ends for a dowel rod.

2 Make a winder from a piece of thick card and two dowel rods. Put the long dowel rod through the box, attaching a handle to one end and a plastic lid to the other.

3 Now make a colour wheel. Paint seven equal segments in the colours of the spectrum. Or try mixing other colours.

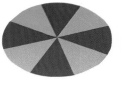

INTRODUCING MAGIC MIRIAM
AND THE
TRANSPORTING BOX

It's incredible! How can the watch be in two places at the same time?

Place the two boxes on the table side by side, with both flaps closed. Ask a member of your audience to lend you a watch (a large one is best). Put the watch into the first box without the mirror. Open the flap and check that the audience can see the watch. Now close that flap and open the other one. The watch has moved!

WHAT YOU NEED
Small plastic or glass mirror
Thick card
Sticky tape
Paint

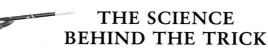

THE SCIENCE
BEHIND THE TRICK

The transporting box works by reflection. The mirror in the second box reflects light from the watch out through the tube. This makes it look as though the watch is actually in the second box. If you look closely, you can see that the figures on the watch face are back to front in the second box, so don't let anyone get too close!

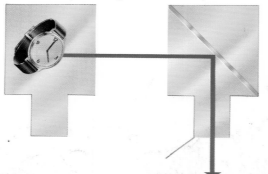

An image of the watch is reflected into the second box and out through the door

1 Make a cube-shaped box from thick card, with one side missing. The mirror should fit diagonally inside, as shown. Cut square holes in the top and front. Make a tube to fit on the front hole, and add a flap at the end.

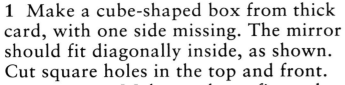

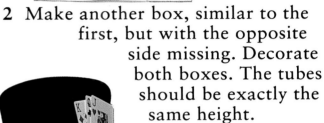

2 Make another box, similar to the first, but with the opposite side missing. Decorate both boxes. The tubes should be exactly the same height.

HINTS AND TIPS

Here are some hints and tips for making your props. Good props will make your act look more professional. So spend time making and decorating your props, and look after them carefully. As well as the special props you need for each trick, try to make some general props such as a waistcoat and magic wand.

Decorate your props with magic shapes cut from coloured paper. Paint bottles and tubes with oil-based paint.

You will need sticky tape and glue to make props. Double-sided tape might also be useful. Thick fabric-based tape is good for joining the edges of boxes together, and it's easy to paint too.

Stencilling is a good way to decorate large areas. Cut magic shapes such as stars and crescent moons out of card. Throw away the shape, but keep the hole! Put the hole over your surface and paint through it with a sponge.

Your act will look extra professional if you make a proper stage set. This is easy if you have a backcloth to hang behind the stage. A large piece of black cloth is most effective. Using silver paint, stencil on stars and moons. The overall effect wil be a set that creates an atmosphere of mystery and magic.

Make your own magician's clothes. Try to find an old hat and waistcoat to decorate. I you can find some silvery material, cut out stars and moons and sow them on. An alternative is to use sequins, or anything else that is shiny and dramatic.

Table

Screen

Cloth

Assistant's table

Make a magician's table by draping a cloth over an ordinary table. Put props out of sight underneath.

GLOSSARY

FILTER A coloured piece of see-through paper that allows certain colours of light to pass through, but not others.

IMAGE The picture of an object which is produced by a lens or mirror. The image is the other way around.

LIGHT A type of wave which can be seen by the eye. Also called visible light.

LINEAR PERSPECTIVE An optical illusion that makes parallel lines appear to meet in the distance.

REFLECTION The bouncing back of light from a surface.

REFRACTION The bending of light when it passes from one transparent substance to another.

MIRROR Piece of shiney glass that can reflect light to form an image.

OPTICAL ILLUSION When the eye is tricked into seeing something that does not really exist.

SPECTRUM The band of rainbow colours that mix together to form "white light".

INDEX